WALKING
ON
DRAGONS

WALKING ON DRAGONS

YOUR AUTHORITY OVER ADVERSITY

STEVE WARMAN

WALKING ON DRAGONS

Published by

LIFEBRIDGE
BOOKS
P.O. BOX 49428
CHARLOTTE, NC 28277

Printed in the United States of America.

CONTENTS

INTRODUCTION

In the stories and folklore that have been passed down through the generations, the great dragon slayers of legendary fame all have one common attribute: an absolutely fearless desire.

This passion may be directed toward different things. For some it was the idea of romance, the knowledge that saving the beautiful princess would result in her display of lifelong love. For others it was the longing to be applauded by the masses for years to come. And some may have been driven by a killer instinct and yearning to save the lives of the villagers who were threatened. Whatever the reason, it was still desire which drove them.

In this book you will meet a new breed of dragon slayer. It may seem unlikely, but this new breed is none other than you!

Perhaps you never imagined in your wildest dreams that you would be called upon to slay a dragon, however, you are the only one who can stop the threat to your village. You have to step up and become the hero. In the process, you will learn how to subdue the dragon under your feet and start walking in victory.

In times past many have allowed this fire-breathing beast to run wild and ruin their lives. Don't allow this to happen, because those you love, including yourself, are depending on you to walk on those dragons.

It's time to step out of the shadows. Be the hero you and God both know you can be. Win the battle for the mind, which will result in the health of your soul and allow you to enjoy a glorious tomorrow. With your foot firmly on the dragon it will be the best future you ever imagined.

The fight is real! It will take a great deal of courage and determination, but you have been given authority. So, lace up your spiritual boots and start walking!

– Steve Warman

ONE

THE PROBLEM WITH DRAGONS

*Thou shalt tread upon the lion
and adder: the young lion and the dragon
shalt thou trample under feet.*
– PSALM 91:13

O kay, I get it! We are supposed to live in authority over our enemy. I am aware of the fact that the lion and the snake represent very real threats —which can hurt and perhaps even destroy us. God has given you and me the power over the all-out assault of the devil in the battle we all face. But, until I began the scriptural search I wasn't sure I understood the dragon.

- What does the Bible mean when it speaks of dragons?
- Is it possible to have authority over these creatures?
- How can I walk on dragons?

All I really knew about dragons derived from tales I heard as a kid which had a high likelihood of being fictitious.

THE PERIL OF THE PRINCESS

One story, which is popular in Europe, is the account of Saint George and The Dragon. The legend takes place in a town called Silene, in Libya, which had a large pond where a plague-bearing dragon dwelled. To appease the creature, the villagers would feed it sheep and maidens. The young women of the village would draw lots to see who would be sacrificed to the dragon.

On one particular day, the lot fell upon the princess of Silene. The king, distraught with grief, told the people they could have all his gold and silver and half of his kingdom if his daughter were spared. However, the citizens, fearing the wrath of the beast, refused. So, the princess was taken to the lake, dressed as a bride, to be fed to the creature.

Saint George, hearing of her plight, rode on horseback to the lake. The princess, trembling, wanted him sent away, but George vowed to remain and fortified himself with the Sign of the Cross.

The dragon reared out of the lake as George and the princess were talking. Saint George gallantly charged on horseback and pierced it with his lance. Then he called to the princess to throw him her waistband, and he put it around the dragon's neck. When this happened, it followed the girl like a dog on a leash.

They led the dragon back into town, where it terrified the people as it approached.

But Saint George told the residents if they would turn to God, the creature would never be able to harm them again. They quickly called on the Lord, and George slew the dragon—and it took four oxcarts to carry the remains out of the city.

CREATIVE FANTASY

It seems practically every culture has at least one story pertaining to dragons—from France to China, Sweden to Japan. Of course, the tales are filled with fantasy and fiction. The stories were concocted in the very fertile soil of some creative mind long ago and have been embellished down through the years.

The accounts include fire-breathing, huge beasts that must be appeased or else they will destroy everything in sight.

In most cases, the dragons of ancient legend could only be stopped by a brave hero.

Think back to your own childhood and you will probably recall one or two dragon tales which still linger in your mind!

SEARCHING FOR THE LEGEND

On a recent road trip with our family we made a

last minute decision to stop on the way home to Detroit at the zoo in Toledo, Ohio. The idea was one that had been lobbied for by our then four year old son, Gavin. And he happily celebrated our last minute decision.

Upon entering the main gate, our nine year old son Myles noticed an advertisement for a dragon exhibit which excited him—so off we went to see what it was all about.

The exhibit was not quite what we had imagined! There were no fire-breathing creatures, no scary looking beasts, just a bunch of reptiles, animals and insects that had the word dragon attached to their name. There were Komodo dragons (a species of lizard which inhabits the island of Komodo in Indonesia), dragon flies, and other dragon-named creatures.

While these delighted our children, it wasn't the animal I had envisioned. I was looking for the dragon of old from the legend, but it was nowhere to be found.

WHAT DOES THE BIBLE SAY?

This brings us to the purpose of what you are

reading. What about biblical dragons? Beyond our legends and stories, do we know anything about them?

A quick search into the scriptures will surface a few references to either a dragon or dragons. The problem arises when we attempt to figure out what the Bible is referring to. The answer can be confusing because it seems that nearly every reference to a dragon in the entire King James Version means something different.

In Psalm 91:13, *"Thou shalt tread upon the lion and adder: the young lion and the dragon shalt thou trample under feet,"* the word dragon spoken of here is translated as being some form of serpent. It is also referred to as this in:

- Isaiah 34:13—*"and it shall be an habitation of dragons."*
- Jeremiah 9:11—*"And I will make Jerusalem heaps, and a den of dragons."*
- Jeremiah 51:37—*"And Babylon shall become heaps, a dwellingplace for dragons, an astonishment, and an hissing, without an inhabitant."*
- Malachi 1:3—*"And I hated Esau, and laid his mountains and his heritage waste for the dragons of the wilderness."*

In other scriptures, we find the word dragon being translated as a wolf, as some sort of sea creature, and as a whale. Dragon is also used in referring to Pharaoh and to Satan. Then there are references where the term is symbolic.

A dragon is described in one place in the Bible as being red in color, in other verses as powerful and poisonous. We read that it swallows its prey, has a mournful voice, it wails, and snuffs up the air. According to the Word, you can find it in the deserted cities, in the dry places, in the wilderness, and in the rivers.

The dragon in scripture is used as an illustration for cruel and evil kings, for enemies of the church, to describe wicked men, the devil, and even wine.

The more research you do on this topic the more confusing it becomes.

You just can't seem to nail the dragon down; it changes from place to place, and switches form and meaning.

A REVELATION

However, as I continued my study, a central theme started to unfold. I began to understand more and more concerning the authority we have as believers to *walk* on dragons—and keep them vanquished under our feet. The psalmist (in Psalm 91:13) is saying that not only will we have the power to walk on the all-out, full, "in your face" attacks of the enemy which we can identify (snakes and lions); but also the things that are small, indescribable, and always moving around.

This revelation brings with it great joy. Because so often it is not the huge confrontations that do us in, rather the minor things we really can't even put our finger on which will cause us to lose direction and ultimately be defeated.

The dragon, even though the word conjures up a large, formidable image, is insignificant in the eyes of God, and should not pose a problem for His children.

Sometimes you cannot even explain to anyone what it is, you just know in your heart it is there. Maybe you *do* know what the dragon is but you are too embarrassed to admit the fact, because it should be small and trivial.

SATAN'S PLAN

Friend, I have discovered it is these hard-to-define dragons which we have such a difficult time overcoming. The enemy of our soul is well aware that if he came to us in a major attack we would immediately run to God and away from him. Because Satan has this knowledge, he very seldom confronts us this way. Hardly ever will he unleash a snake or lion, he just keeps sending dragons, things we can't quite figure out, that are hard to explain and should never be a problem, but sadly are.

Remember: just as sure as we were promised authority over the lion and snake in Psalm 91, we are also promised command and dominion over that dragon.

In the chapters which follow we will identify a few dragons, and perhaps it will spur your mind to name one or two which have been affecting you.

In the process, get ready to strap on your boots and start walking in the victory which God intends for us. Are you ready?

Two

TREADING ON LIONS

Without question, a lion is an extremely dangerous animal that can become a real threat to your well being. It is referred to in our foundation scripture: *"Thou shalt tread upon the lion and adder: the young lion and the dragon shalt thou trample under feet"* (Psalm 91:13).

I may not be an expert on lions, but what I do know is that you do not, under any circumstances ever want to tangle with one of these ferocious beasts. One swipe of his mighty paw can absolutely rip a human to shreds. In its natural habitat we fear the lion, and well we should.

You just don't find very many people with a lion living in their apartment or chained up in their backyard as a pet. Most of us only see them at the zoo or as a part of a circus act. The reason being, a lion must be handled and kept by a person who is trained and has the ability to control its wild nature.

It seems to me that when I am looking at a lion on the other side of a cage, the eyes of this magnificent animal look beyond me. It is almost as if the caged beast is longing to leave the confines of captivity and go back to the wild where he reigns as "king of the jungle." This animal was never meant to live in captivity, rather to roam freely.

"WHAT ARE YOUR CREDENTIALS?"

In the scriptures we read about the awesome power of the lion. When David trekked to the encampment of Israel to bring bread, corn and cheese to his brothers and their captains (1 Samuel 17), he quickly noticed there was no battle, only a giant who yelled out taunts daily.

David was so upset by the fact Goliath mocked his God and his nation, that he began an inquiry which eventually brought him into the presence of King Saul. Then, while Saul was trying to make a decision on whether or not to send this boy to fight a trained giant, something interesting occurs. Saul questions David, "What are your credentials for this fight?"

———————※———————

Saul must have been thinking, "How could I ever send this boy out against Goliath?"

When he continued, "Why should I send you?" David replied: *"Thy servant kept his father's sheep, and there came a lion, and a bear, and took a lamb out of the flock: And I went out after him, and smote him, and delivered it out of his mouth: and when he arose against me, I caught him by his beard, and smote him, and slew him. Thy servant slew both the lion and the bear: and this uncircumcised Philistine shall be as one of them, seeing he hath defied the armies of the living God. David said moreover, The Lord that delivered me out of the paw of the lion, and out of the paw of the bear, he will deliver me out of the hand of this Philistine"* (1 Samuel 17:34-37).

PREPARATION FOR THE BATTLE

We don't know what species of bear David killed. He didn't say if it was a black bear, grizzly bear, or polar bear, but I guarantee you it wasn't Winnie the Pooh! It was a *dangerous* bear.

I'm also not sure what kind of lion David killed. He did not mention if it was a mountain or African lion, but we are pretty sure it was not Simba! It was a very ferocious beast.

It is interesting to note that Saul let David fight the Philistine champion with no real battle experience. The decision was based only on his exploits with the bear and the lion.

PUNISHMENT FOR DISOBEDIENCE

We see the power of the lion again in 1 Kings 13. I love how *The Message* translation tells the story:

And then this happened: Just as Jeroboam was at the Altar, about to make an offering, a holy man came from Judah by God's command and preached (these were God' orders) to the Altar: "Altar, Altar! God's message! 'A son will be born into David's family named Josiah. The priests from the shrines who are making offerings on you, he will sacrifice—on you! Human bones burned on you!"' At the same time he announced a sign: "This is the proof God gives —the Altar will split into pieces and the holy offerings spill into the dirt" (1 Kings 13:1-3).

*W*hen *the king heard the message the holy man preached against the Altar at Bethel, he reached out to grab him, yelling, "Arrest him!" But his arm was paralyzed and hung useless. At the same time the Altar broke apart and the holy offerings all spilled into the dirt—the very sign the holy man had announced by God's command. The king pleaded with the holy man, "Help me! Pray to your God for the healing of my arm." The holy man prayed for him and the king's arm was healed—as good as new!* (verses 4-6).

*T*hen *the king invited the holy man, "Join me for a meal; I have a gift for you." The holy man*

told the king, "Not on your life! You couldn't
pay me enough to get me to sit down with you
at a meal in this place. I'm here under God's
orders, and he commanded, 'Don't eat a crumb,
don't drink a drop, and don't go back the way
you came.'" Then he left by a different road
than the one on which he had walked to Bethel
(verses 7-10).

*T*here was an old prophet who lived in Bethel.
His sons came and told him the story of what
the holy man had done that day in Bethel, told
him everything that had happened and what
the holy man had said to the king. Their father
said, "Which way did he go?" His sons pointed
out the road that the holy man from Judah had
taken. He told his sons, "Saddle my donkey."
When they had saddled it, he got on and rode
after the holy man. He found him sitting under
an oak tree. He asked him, "Are you the holy
man who came from Judah?" "Yes, I am," he
said. "Well, come home with me and have a
meal." "Sorry, I can't do that," the holy man

said. "I can neither go back with you nor eat with you in this country. I'm under strict orders from God: 'Don't eat a crumb; don't drink a drop; and don't come back the way you came.'" But he said, "I am also a prophet, just like you. And an angel came to me with a message from God: 'Bring him home with you, and give him a good meal!'" But the man was lying (verses 11-18).

So the holy man went home with him and they had a meal together. There they were, sitting at the table together, when the word of God came to the prophet who had brought him back. He confronted the holy man who had come from Judah: "God's word to you: You disobeyed God's command; you didn't keep the strict orders your God gave you; you came back and sat down to a good meal in the very place God told you, 'Don't eat a crumb; don't drink a drop.' For that you're going to die far from home and not be buried in your ancestral tomb" (verses 19-22).

When the meal was over, the prophet who had brought him back saddled his donkey for him. Down the road a way, a lion met him and killed him. His corpse lay crumpled on the road, the lion on one side and the donkey on the other. Some passersby saw the corpse in a heap on the road, with the lion standing guard beside it. They went to the village where the old prophet lived and told what they had seen. When the prophet who had gotten him off track heard it, he said, "It's the holy man who disobeyed God's strict orders. God turned him over to the lion who knocked him around and killed him, just as God had told him" (verses 23-26).

The Almighty used this lion as punishment for the disobedient man of God.

INTO A DEN OF LIONS

The king of the jungle is a scary creature, and we even find it used as a form of capital punishment to kill those who broke the law.

In Daniel's day a group of jealous men who were out to get him convinced King Darius to pass a decree that anyone who prayed to a god or mortal besides Darius for thirty days would be thrown into a den of lions (Daniel 6).

The princes and regents could not deal with their own jealousy of Daniel, his success, and the fact it seemed the king listened to his advice. They knew exactly what they were doing when they convinced Darius to pass this decree, they were confident Daniel would not go thirty days without prayer; as a matter of fact he would not go *one* day without talking to his God.

Perhaps you know the story. Daniel prayed, the king threw him in a lions den, but the Lord sent His angel to shut the lions mouths and Daniel came out unscathed.

We serve a God who will absolutely come down to the lions den for us, if we will make a stand for Him.

Not even a hungry lion has an appetite for a praying man!

CLAIM GOD'S PROMISE

The apostle Peter admonishes us: *"Be sober, be vigilant; because your adversary the devil, as a roaring lion, walketh about, seeking whom he may devour"* (1 Peter 5:8).

Yes, it is true that Satan is like a wild beast, stalking his prey looking for an opportunity to totally destroy you; but God has given you power over him. I heard someone say that the word "may" in the above verse speaks to them of permission. In other words the lion can only devour you if you *allow* him to.

Satan has no authority over the child of God unless we give it to him.

I refuse to grant him permission to destroy me because I have a mighty promise that says "I will tread on lions"—and I claim this in Jesus' name.

Don't be conquered by the lion! With God's help, turn the tables on him and destroy his hold on your life. You may be facing a vicious and ferocious attack of the enemy right now, but you are not to be walked on by the lion; you are to walk on him!

Since you've already strapped on your spiritual boots, start walking! God will meet you in the lions lair and help you every step of the way.

THREE

STEPPING ON SNAKES

I can understand why the psalmist would be inspired to write about the authority given to us as the ability to walk on snakes: *"Thou shalt tread upon the lion and adder: the young lion and the dragon shalt thou trample under feet"* (Psalm 91:13).

To me this represents ultimate power, because I loathe and despise snakes. I do not want to ever hold, handle, be close to or even *see* a snake. I have a very real fear of these reptiles because to me they symbolize a dangerous threat. So, the writer of the psalms really speaks to me personally when he says that I will have power to overcome the snake.

SLITHERING IN THE YARD

I grew up in Northeast Arkansas, in a town called

Blytheville. My father has been the pastor of a church there for most of my life and it was an ideal place for me and my brothers to grow up.

Blytheville is a town situated in the middle of thousands and thousands of acres of cotton fields. Our home was built in a subdivision about three miles outside of town and was literally surrounded by and endless vista of white balls of cotton.

I also remember there were a lot of snakes in Arkansas. Big, bad, poisonous ones everywhere— water moccasins, blue racers, cotton mouths, copperheads, king snakes (which I am told are not poisonous, but I don't care), and the list goes on. Since we saw all of these species in our yard, one would think that over time I would lose my fear because I had seen so many, but this never happened. I am afraid of snakes to this day and still have a phobia about them.

TOO FRIGHTENED TO HELP!

There is a distinct memory from this time in my life, one of which I am rather ashamed. I recall one day coming home with my mother and brothers, and for some reason we did not enter the house through the garage, but went around to the front door.

As my mother was about to walk inside, we noticed a large snake resting above the door frame.

I am embarrassed to admit this, because I was at the time a grown teenager and so was Mark, my younger brother. But my dear mother ended up taking care of the snake herself with a garden hoe—all because I was too petrified to do anything about the situation.

PANDEMONIUM!

Once, as a young, single man I was invited to speak at a retreat for youth. One afternoon during the event it was decided we would go to the local zoo as a field trip. When we arrived, there was immediate agreement for us to visit the snake house. I was young, single and cool, and was not about to expose my fear in front of this group. So I acquiesced to the majority's insistence and went into the snake house.

The minute we stepped into the exhibit I knew it would be a rough day! The place was dark and cold. Not only that, but the glass cages which housed the snakes were stacked three high and were on both sides of the passage way. The problem with this setup was that I knew there was no way possible for me to keep my eyes on all the snakes at the same time; however I was determined to try.

As we walked deeper into the building my fear escalated. What made matters worse was the fact that on each glass cage there was a small bronze plaque which told the name of the serpent. The plaque had at the top the English name identifying the snake, but under that was a Latin form of the same name and I don't remember exactly what the plaque said, but the Latin words looked ominous to me—like *bitus handus*, or *bitus footus.* This was freaking me out!

I know the risk is remote for a snake to escape from the confines of a zoo and terrorize the patrons, but there is always a first time and I felt this might be it.

I tried desperately to keep my eyes focused on all the snakes at the same time. In my zeal, I didn't notice that one of the zoo workers had dragged a garden hose across the pathway. Out of all the places on the planet for my foot to come down, you guessed it, it landed right on the garden hose—and pandemonium broke loose in the snake house!

I thought they were going to have to call 911 to get me out of that place. I hate snakes!

I PRAYED!

A few years ago while visiting one of our churches in Ghana, West Africa, the pastor Nana Boacie-Yiadom, wanted my father-in-law and I to accompany him to a place where he prayed. This location was out in the fields, so when the vehicle stopped, the women stayed behind as the men started walking down this little trail out into the fields to Nana's prayer place.

As we marched single file, Nana in front, Roland Baker in the middle, and me bringing up the rear, suddenly between me and my father-in-law across the path appeared the biggest snake I have ever seen in my life! I never made it to the place of prayer. I did my praying on the way back to sit in the car with the women. Let me reiterate: I literally despise snakes!

THE ROD BECAME A SERPENT

One of my Bible heroes is Moses. When God called this man in the wilderness to go into Egypt and tell Pharaoh, "Let my people go," Moses had an experience at the burning bush (Exodus 3).

It was not so much that the bush was burning which captured Moses' attention, it was how the bush *kept* burning and was not consumed which caused Moses to say, "I will turn aside and see this great sight."

God began to speak to Moses out of the bush concerning his assignment in Egypt, and he asked the Lord, "Who will I say has sent me? I can't just go in and announce I have been out talking to a bush in the wilderness and the bush said 'Let my people go.'"

The Almighty replied, *"Thus shalt thou say unto the children of Israel, I AM hath sent me unto you"* (verse 14).

However, Moses was still apprehensive and needed a little more to go on. Exodus 4:1-3 will show you why

Moses is my Bible hero: *"And Moses answered and said, But, behold, they will not believe me, nor hearken unto my voice: for they will say, The Lord hath not appeared unto thee. And the Lord said unto him, What is that in thine hand? And he said, A rod. And he said, Cast it on the ground. And he cast it on the ground, and it became a serpent; and Moses fled from before it."*

Even if this were my first time reading the Bible, I would like Moses right there and then; I would know without a shadow of doubt this man would do great things. Why? Because Moses had good common sense!

When the rod hit the ground and became a slithering serpent, Moses did what anybody with good sense would do, He ran!

A snake poses a very real and present danger!

THE MIRACLE

In Exodus chapter seven Moses had an encounter with Pharaoh which was quite interesting. Moses and

Aaron went in to see Pharaoh and the Egyptian leader wanted to see a miracle performed by them. So Aaron threw down his rod and it became a serpent. (This rod thing would be freaking me out!)

When Aaron's rod turned into a snake, the magicians of Pharaoh threw their rods down and they also became snakes. Then Aaron's serpent swallowed all of their serpents. That was one bad snake! I know it was in God's plan and it helped free the Israelites out of Egypt, but I am sorry, a rod that becomes a snake which can eat up all the other snakes in the room...that scares me to death!

SNAKE HANDLING?

We see how very real the threat of a serpent's bite is in Numbers 21. Moses had led the people out of Egypt, but they were growing impatient with their journey and began to complain against both God and Moses.

The Bible records how *"the Lord sent fiery serpents among the people, and they bit the people; and much people of Israel died"* (verse 6).

These venomous reptiles were unleashed as

punishment for their actions, bringing death.

*I know there are certain people
in this country who handle snakes as
a part of their religion. Let me assure
you I am not one of them.*

The only way I want to handle a snake is with a ten foot pole!

Yet, Jesus made this statement before He ascended back to heaven: *"And these signs shall follow them that believe; In my name shall they cast out devils; they shall speak with new tongues; They shall take up serpents; and if they drink any deadly thing, it shall not hurt them; they shall lay hands on the sick, and they shall recover"* (Mark 16:17-18).

I interpret the words concerning taking up serpents and drinking any deadly thing to mean if it happens accidentally then God will take care of you—as the apostle Paul experienced while gathering sticks to build a fire on the island of Malta. Scripture records, *"when Paul had gathered a bundle of sticks, and laid them on the fire, there came a viper out of the heat, and fastened on his hand. And when the barbarians saw the venomous beast hang on his hand, they said among themselves, No doubt this man is a murderer, whom, though he hath escaped the sea, yet vengeance suffereth not to live. And he shook off the beast into the fire, and felt no harm"* (Acts 28:3-5).

It was God's protection—and it caused those who witnessed this event to believe on the Lord Paul served.

YOUR AUTHORITY

If the scripture references to the danger of snakes is not enough for you, then consider the account of John Sudworth, the BBC correspondent who reported from New Delhi on September 10, 2006, that approximately 50,000 people a year die in India from snake bites.

My friend, a snake poses a true threat, but the promise of God through the psalmist is that we will be able to walk on serpents.

This divine assurance is very simple and plain. We will have the power to overcome every single attack of the enemy. There will be no offensive onslaught from the devil that can defeat us.

———————— 🐉 ————————

*God has given us the authority
to walk over our adversaries.*

We can rejoice in this knowledge when we are faced with the outright, "on the offensive" attack of Satan. All we have to do is remember that we are to step on the enemy instead of him trampling on us.

SATAN'S DESIRE

Ever since mankind's first encounter with the serpent in the Garden of Eden, when Adam and Eve succumbed to his lies, God has given us the right and authority to crush the head of our enemy.

Here is what the Almighty said to the serpent: *"Because you have done this, Cursed are you above all the livestock and all the wild animals! You will crawl on your belly and you will eat dust all the days of your life. And I will put enmity between you and the woman, and between your offspring and hers; he will crush your head, and you will strike his heel"* (Genesis 3:14-15 NIV).

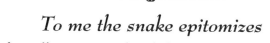

To me the snake epitomizes the all-out attack of the enemy against our lives and our faith.

It depicts the desire of Satan to destroy us, just as happened in the garden at the beginning of time. The lives of Adam, Eve, and subsequently our own lives, were affected because of this confrontation.

YOUR SPIRITUAL ROUNDUP

Every year somewhere around the second weekend in March, the Jaycees of Sweetwater, Texas, host a Rattlesnake Roundup. It is reported that since its inception in 1958, there have been over 225,000 pounds of rattlers captured. Thousands of people flock into Sweetwater, swelling the population to twice its normal size. These individuals participate in all kinds of events including, the roundup parade, the Miss Snake Charmer Pageant, Rattlesnake Sighting Bus

Tours, and much more. The weekend offers many activities, but the original purpose for the roundup is fulfilled when all of the snakes are brought in to the Nolan County Coliseum where they are weighed and the captors are rewarded.

I must confess that I am not sure how I feel about the roundup; I do know that I will not be participating!

However, I believe it is time for you and me to go out into the canyons and deserts of our spiritual lives and round up every deceit of the enemy and win the victory. Let's do what the Word has promised: *"And the God of peace will crush Satan under your feet shortly. The grace of our Lord Jesus Christ be with you. Amen.* (Romans 16:20).

With this awesome assurance, we truly *can* start stepping on snakes!

FOUR

CASTING DOWN DRAGONS

Make no mistake; you are fighting a battle. You may not be deployed on behalf of the armed forces and may not own a physical weapon or wear a uniform, but you are engaged in a mighty conflict.

The Bible tells us, *"For though we walk in the flesh, we do not war after the flesh: (For the weapons of our warfare are not carnal, but mighty through God to the pulling down of strong holds;) Casting down imaginations, and every high thing that exalteth itself against the knowledge of God, and bringing into captivity every thought to the obedience of Christ"* (2 Corinthians 10:3-5).

I fear that many of us have become involved in the

wrong battle. Somehow we have been duped into believing that our enemy is a natural one. It is not; our real foe can't be seen with our eyes or heard with our ears. In addition, we cannot defeat this opponent with a military battle plan. There is no bomb or grenade you can implode to stop this foe.

Your adversary is not another person and does not bunker in the sands of some distant desert.

Your enemy lurks in the place where it is hardest to reach; it lives in your mind.

I guess you could say you are fighting against yourself. You are in the midst of a war in conflict with your own thoughts—fighting everything that exalts itself against the knowledge of God.

DON'T FIGHT THE WRONG WAR

Let me be totally honest and confess I have spent much of my life fighting the wrong battle. It is so easy to do, because no one wants to admit that what causes them the greatest harm is the thing hidden in their own heart. Subsequently many of us are spinning our wheels, wasting our time, embroiled in the wrong conflict.

It seems that our society encourages us to divide into groups. And this has produced a war in which we should never be involved. For example, we are divided politically and religiously. We are placed into different camps economically, socially, educationally, and on and on it goes, one group pitted against another.

For awhile, all of this can divert our attention from what is really bothering us, but the relief is short lived and soon we are left to face the biggest and worst enemy of all, our imagination.

While we have been busy pulling down each other, we should have been concentrating on conquering strongholds. While we have been casting down our brothers and sisters, we should have been confronting imaginations. We tend to look for the low hanging fruit, the "easy pickings," but what we need to go after is the high things which exalt themselves against Christ and His Kingdom.

The wisest thing to do right now is to settle in your heart and mind that the war you need to wage is not outward; it lies inward. This is where the victory will be won—and lay the groundwork for tomorrow's success.

IDENTIFY THE ENEMY

I constantly pray for the ability to see and address my own faults. One of the most detestable things in the world is watching someone point out everyone else's shortcomings, yet they remain oblivious to their own. I do not want to be the person who tells everybody else what to do as though I have it all together, yet all the while I have gaping wounds in my own character.

I struggle with imaginations as much as anybody, but praise God, I am on my way; at least I have identified my enemy. Now I just want to help and encourage as many as I possibly can to do the same in their own lives.

Let's go to work on these imaginations, because we can't heal others if we are not personally healthy.

We can't help those around us when we are totally burdened down with our own baggage. So let's capture our dragons and place them under our feet so we can walk in victory.

YOUR "SURVIVAL KNIFE"

The name of this game is Spiritual Survival.

Someone once told me, "You have to survive until you can thrive"—and this is absolutely true.

When I think survival mode, I can't help but reflect on a pop trend of the 1980s, the decade in which I grew up. Many Americans gave their children a gift which was popular in homes across the nation. This item was a survival knife, and I was one of the lucky recipients.

This gadget is basically a dull knife with a camouflaged handle and a compass on the end. I guess the compass was there in case one day we got on the wrong bus at school and found ourselves stranded in Outer Mongolia; we would then be able to find our way home!

When you unscrewed the compass on the end of

the handle it revealed a hollow area and inside were all of the items one would need in order to exist in the elements. This packet, called the "survival knife kit" came complete with matches, fishing hooks and line, a metal wire saw, and maybe even a button and some thread.

Matches to start a fire and keep away hypothermia. Fishing hooks and line to feed yourself (if you happened to be stranded by a bass lake). Button's and thread so you could look sharp while you survived! The wire saw was provided so you could cut down trees. I suppose it was possible, but it would take you many days. If you were strong and persistent you would eventually have wood for your fire.

LOOK INSIDE!

Let me give you a survival knife for today—a spiritual one, because I am more interested in your spiritual welfare than anything else.

The compass of this knife points to Jesus Christ, the author and finisher of our faith; if you are going to endure until the end you will need to come into the presence of Jesus. Never try to live one day without Him.

Also in this knife is the packet which contains exactly what you need for your spiritual journey. Look inside and there it is! Faith to keep going, the Word to light your path, prayer to give you victory and determination to finish the course. You will need all of these tools if you are going to defeat the dragons hiding in the darkness.

AVAILABLE POWER

You have many effective weapons at your disposal. And though they are not carnal, nor the munitions you would normally think of, they are extremely powerful.

The equipment God gives for spiritual warfare is mighty through Him.

This is important. Such weapons are useless when they are employed outside of the Lord's favor, strength and anointing, but when activated through God, they pull down strongholds.

The problem you thought you could never overcome will be defeated if you use the arsenal God places at your disposal. Opposition you never felt powerful enough to attack will now fall swiftly at your feet. All of this happens when you identify who you are and see the adversity for what it is, merely a distraction that cannot defeat you but can cause you to defeat yourself.

The greatest armies in the world pale in comparison to the Christian who understands the power available to him or her.

The largest cache of weapons ever assembled does not match the potential of one committed, determined believer. You are powerful, overcoming and victorious, so stop cowering in fear and start moving forward in trust and belief.

The faith-filled life drives the dragons crazy, because they know their days are numbered in the mind of a spiritual warrior.

THE REAL BATTLE

When the apostle Paul talks of this warfare it seems he is not even referring to what we normally consider when we think of a battle of the spirit. The term "spiritual warfare" quickly conjures images of a great clash between Satan, sin, and evil on one side and God, good, and righteousness on the other.

Our thoughts slip into seeing an enormous conflict just above our heads between angels and demons. God's angelic messengers wear shiny silver helmets and swords, while the demons are draped in black and smell of sulphur.

I am not saying this never happens, indeed it may. It seems, however, that we miss the point when we over-spiritualize this particular passage. Paul is telling us that the most significant spiritual battle is not against the devil and his imps, but rather with our own mind. These imaginations are what I call dragons. They are the thoughts you can't nail down. You're not sure where they even come from; you only know they exist and are present.

"THE PLACE OF THE SKULL"

The bottom line to all of this is the conflict is fought and won or lost in our mind. If we can win in our thought life we can triumph over the devil.

Don't spend too much time worrying over the spiritual realm. God will be victorious.

———— ❦ ————

Good will win and light will conquer darkness.

However, we do need to be concerned over the battle taking place in our own mind.

Someone pointed out to me how appropriate it was that when Jesus was crucified it was at Golgotha, "the place of the skull." It is noteworthy the crucifixion occurred on a skull-shaped hill, because really the war for the soul is fought in the mind. It is true that "Jesus paid it all" on the cross, but now it is our turn to cooperate with Him and allow Him to give us the victory in our own lives.

THE DANGER OF UNCONTROLLABLE THOUGHTS

The foes that will conquer you are listed in 2 Corinthians 10:5—they are "imaginations," "high things," and "every thought." Stop for a moment and consider this fact: you don't just suddenly get involved in an activity that is not pleasing to God, you start by wrong thinking first, then you act. However, when you have a "saved mind," your soul will prosper.

Focus for a moment on imaginations and realize they will absolutely destroy you if you let them. You can sit around and dwell on all the negative aspects of living. Soon, the dragons will convince you that people don't like you and you will begin to notice those who pass by without speaking. Before long it is settled in your mind, "No one likes me!"

The dragons will then begin to create all sorts of scenarios that can result in your failure, and you will eventually find yourself saying, "I am a loser!"

Unruly thoughts will soon create emotions you can't seem to control and these dragons will ruin everything if you let them. Church services come and go, the pastor speaks, but you can't even hear what he says because of these uncontrollable images. The choir raises their voices in song and the worship experience happens, but you can't participate because you are ruled by your thoughts. Everyone else is living a joyous life while you slink backwards because you are under the thumb of these dragons.

MAKE AN ARREST!

We have all struggled at one point with something the knowledge of Christ says is not so but, we give into the intimidation of our thoughts. No, it's not the vicious outright attack of the enemy that destroys us, it is our silly imagination.

Struggle no more. Identify the true enemy and go after it.

This is the time for a giant arrest!

- Every evil thought needs to go to jail.
- Every negative concept needs to be placed into captivity.
- Every thought that brings with it doubt and fear should be locked up.

Apprehend your wayward thinking and make a citizen's arrest. Tell everything that exalts itself against God, "You can't live free anymore! Negative, fearful, doubtful, ungodly thoughts—your days of running loose in my mind and torturing my existence are over!

Right now, put on your armor, grab your sword and let's climb up to the high places in your mind and emotions and chase those dragons away.

Every thought, every dragon must come into the obedience and control of the Lord Jesus Christ.

It's time to tell the dragons, "I will live a surrendered life. I will bring everything about me, including my thoughts into submission to Christ."

Yes, you can enjoy a God-controlled journey, one that is under the authority of the Holy Spirit.

A FIGHT YOU CAN WIN

I know it is not going to be an easy task to capture your dragons. After all they have elevated themselves to the place where they boldly stand against you and your knowledge of Christ. Some of these have been hiding in your heart and mind for a very long time and they have claimed a high place of refuge to grow and flourish. It will be a major skirmish since these evil opponents have been feeding off of your emotions so long that they have become huge, fire-breathing behemoths.

The enemies of your soul will not give up without a fight, but you have the armor of God. So boldly open the cage door and command every one of them to flee in the powerful name of Jesus.

FIVE

THE DRAGON OF ANGER

We are living in a violent, infuriated culture. Everywhere we look there is an abundance of anger. It is prevalent in music, the movies, television, radio and newspapers. It seems that everyone is upset over one issue or another.

Daily doses of news reports seem to verify this fact. Murder, rape, violent crime, and a general disregard for the feelings of our fellow man are constantly leading the headlines. Teenagers and children intentionally start a fight so that the video footage can be captured, bringing them a few seconds of notoriety.

We even see the effects of the grip of wrath in our elected officials. It appears that the days of disagreeing on an issue yet remaining cordial to each other is a remnant of the past as the people in our nation's capital become more and more personal and vengeful.

Perhaps this generation of national leaders should take heed to the advice of a couple of our founding fathers. Benjamin Franklin stated, "Anger is never without a reason, but seldom with a good one." And Thomas Jefferson advised, "When angry, count to ten before you speak; if very angry, an hundred."

This wise counsel is being ignored daily in our bitter, spiteful world.

"COOL YOUR PIPES!"

The dragon of anger is on the loose and it appears millions are listening to his lies. This enemy is not only having an impact, but it is being promoted by certain segments of society. An entire genre of media and entertainment seems to be wholly sold on the idea of pushing outrage and violence on our kids.

Yes, the anger is running wild and will try to convince you that the "out of control" emotions you display are both common and acceptable. "It is perfectly natural" is the message this dragon constantly sends.

While it is true that anger is an emotion which surfaces quite naturally and you cannot necessarily control your feelings, let me be very clear: you may not be able to harness how you feel, but you can take charge over your *response* to your emotions.

I pray you will avoid the trap of giving into this dragon and doing something you will regret for the rest of your life. The prisons are crowded with individuals who could not control their temper. Events happen so quickly, many times without warning, and before you know it you have engaged in a response that will forever change the course of your life.

Sadly, lives are being destroyed hourly by this dragon. Don't let yours be one of them.

The psalmist writes, *"Cease from anger, and forsake wrath: fret not thyself in any wise to do evil"* (Psalm 37:8). *The Message* translates this scripture in an awesome way, *"Bridle your anger, trash your wrath, cool your pipes—it only makes things worse. "*

YOU'RE AT RISK

It is interesting how the scriptures teach us something that science will come to verify much later. According to researchers at the University of Pittsburgh and the University of Helsinki, children and adolescents with hostile responses are also placing themselves at increased risk of developing metabolic syndrome—a precursor to adult heart disease, according to a study in *Health Psychology*, published by the American Psychological Association (APA).

The publication also included this data: Using a sample of 774 older white men (average age was 60) from the Normative Aging Study, lead researcher Raymond Niaura, Ph.D., and colleagues sought to determine whether hostility was an independent influence or a contributing factor in CHD (coronary heart disease) development. Hostility levels, blood lipids, fasting insulin, blood pressure, body measurement index (BMI), weight-hip ratio (WHR), diet, alcohol intake, smoking and education attainment were assessed over a three year period beginning in 1986.

Incidences of CHD were more common in those with higher levels of hostility then those with other risk factors such as high cholesterol, alcohol intake or smoking tobacco, said Dr. Niaura. In this sample of older men with high levels of hostility, 5.8 percent (45) experienced at least one episode of CHD during their involvement with the NAS study. According to the authors, hostility is associated with and predicts incidents of coronary heart disease above and beyond the influence of known risk factors that include blood lipid profiles, sociodemographic characteristics, alcohol consumption and smoking. Specifically, HDL-cholesterol levels did significantly protect against CHD but hostility levels predicted incidences of CHD independent of the protective effect of HDL.

Simply stated, uncontrolled anger is dangerous for you, your health, and everyone around you.

It is extremely important that you learn to take charge of your anger before it takes charge of you. Don't allow it to devastate your future.

CLOSE THE DOOR!

The book of Ephesians gives us insight into the proper way to deal with our wrath. Paul does not teach that it is sin, rather he counsels how uncontrolled rage which is not properly dealt with is a trespass in God's sight. He tells us, *"Be ye angry, and sin not: let not the sun go down upon your wrath: Neither give place to the devil"* (Ephesians 4:26-27).

It is clear that anger which is not bridled and dealt with gives the devil an opening and allows him to find a place to reside inside you.

Many of the things that trip us up in our walk with God are the result of an anger issue. Try this: instead of allowing such feelings to eat away at you and give the devil a foothold in your life, direct your negative emotions toward your true enemy, Satan. Take action to kill his influence—activities such as prayer, fasting, giving, forgiving, and blessing others will help you accomplish this.

Long ago, Thomas Aquinas wrote, "Anger is the name of a passion. A passion of the sensitive appetite is good in so far as it is regulated by reason, whereas it is evil if it set the order of reason aside."

It has also been noted that anger is *energy*, so harness it and make it work for you.

STAND ON THE WORD

Whenever the dragon of anger tries to seek a corner in your mind and emotions, get your Bible out and read these scriptures. I know they will make a positive difference:

- *"He that is slow to anger is better than the mighty; and he that ruleth his spirit than he that taketh a city"* (Proverbs 16:32).
- *"But I say to you, That whosover is angry with his brother without cause shall be in danger of the judgment"* (Matthew 5:22).
- *"Let all bitterness, and wrath, and anger, and clamour, and evil speaking, be put away from you, with all malice: And be ye kind one to*

*another, tenderhearted, forgiving one another,
even as God for Christ's sake hath forgiven you"*
(Ephesians 4:31-32).

Relegate the dragon of anger to the place he belongs—under your feet!

SIX

THE DRAGON OF DECEIT

Early on Sunday morning, December 7, 1941, at about 7:55 A.M. local Hawaii Time, Captain Fuchida of the Imperial Japanese Navy gave the command that launched an attack on the naval station at Pearl Harbor. The first wave of bombardment brought 181 Japanese planes. This was followed 30 minutes later by a second wave of 170 planes.

They attacked military airfields at the same time they hit the fleet anchored in Pearl Harbor. The Navy air bases at Ford Island and Kaneohe Bay, the Marine airfield at Ewa and the Army Air Corps fields at Bellows, Wheeler and Hickam were all bombed and strafed as other elements of the enemy force began their assaults on the ships moored in Pearl Harbor. The purpose of the simultaneous attacks was to destroy the American planes before they could rise to intercept the Japanese.

At about 8:10 A.M., the USS *Arizona* was mortally wounded by an armor-piercing bomb which ignited the ship's forward ammunition magazine. The resulting explosion and fire killed 1,177 crewmen, the greatest loss of life on any ship. When the blitz ended shortly before 10:00 A.M., less than two hours after it began, the American forces had paid a fearful price. Twenty-one ships of the U.S. Pacific Fleet were sunk or damaged.

Aircraft losses were 188 destroyed and 159 damaged, the majority hit before they had a chance to take off. American dead numbered 2,403. This figure included 68 civilians, most of them killed by improperly fused anti-aircraft shells landing in Honolulu. There were 1,178 military and civilian wounded.

The tragic and unprecedented news quickly hit the streets. The cabinet rushed to the White House. President Roosevelt called a special session of congress and America was thrown into the midst of a terrible and disastrous war. Unfortunately for our nation, the attack on Pearl Harbor took us totally by surprise. We simply were not ready for such a brutal and vicious assault.

ANOTHER TRAGEDY

Nearly 60 years later it came again. This time I would be around to see the effects of a ruthless attack on innocent people. Just before 9:00 A.M. Eastern standard time.

I was sitting at the desk in my office at church, when someone came by and said that a plane had just crashed into the World Trade Center.

Because the information was so sparse, I assumed that perhaps a small plane had veered off course and this was a minor episode. I continued working. Until, moments later when the staff member returned to let me know another plane had crashed into the other tower.

We immediately began to hunt news sources and spent the remainder of the day looking on in disbelief and horror as the events that shall forever be clear in my memory began to unfold. September 11, 2001, was simply an unbelievable and tragic day.

The towers, which had taken six years and eight months to build, were destroyed in just one hour and forty-two minutes. The buildings had been designed to handle the crash of a Boeing 707 moving at 180 M.P.H., but the two Boeing 767 jets hit the towers at 470 M.P.H. and 590 M.P.H. and they plunged deep into the structures, creating havoc and chaos for everyone inside.

When American Airlines flight 11 hit the north tower it caused an earthquake-like tremor that registered 0.9 in magnitude. The fires ignited by the jet fuel heated the steel up to 1800 degrees—and soon the steel lost its strength and the towers came crumbling down. When the north tower collapsed it registered as an earthquake in magnitude of 2.3 on the Richter scale 21 miles away. And when it was all over we discovered that nearly 3,000 people had lost their lives.

One company alone, Cantor Fitzgerald, lost 658

employees that day. A total of 343 New York City Firefighters, 60 of whom were off duty, lost their lives. Sixty police officers responding to the emergency also died.

Simply put, this tragedy came upon us because we were not expecting the attack.

The sad truth remains: no matter how much trust we put into our government and military they cannot keep us safe from every act of aggression.

We have spent billions upon billions of dollars to train and prepare our military to defend us, yet the enemies of our nation are searching at this very moment for other ways to infiltrate and inflict terror.

LULLED TO SLEEP

This reminds me of the greatest adversary we will ever face—the enemy of our soul. He attacks us when we least expect it and are totally unprepared to defend ourselves. This is why we cannot lean on the arm of flesh.

The prophet Jeremiah proclaimed: *"Cursed is the strong one who depends on mere humans, Who thinks he can make it on muscle alone and sets God aside as dead weight. He's like a tumbleweed on the prairie, out of touch with the good earth. He lives rootless and aimless in a land where nothing grows"* (Jeremiah 17:5-6 TM).

We are facing a strong spiritual onslaught, yet many of us are being lulled to sleep.

The dragon that says we can thwart any assault by our own human reasoning and ingenuity has caused us to have false confidence and lose our focus.

STRENGTH AND COURAGE

We must heed the lesson Hezekiah learned in his day.

As recorded in 2 Chronicles 32, when an Assyrian king named Sennacherib launched an unexpected attack on Judah and it became clear to Hezekiah that he would not stop until he had taken Jerusalem,

Hezekiah went to work.

He immediately cut off the possibility of a water supply for the Assyrian army. Hezekiah built weapons for his people and put together a force to stand against this military offensive.

When all the troops were prepared, Hezekiah called the people to the public square and made one of the most profound statements ever recorded: *"Be strong and courageous, be not afraid nor dismayed for the king of Assyria, nor for all the multitude that is with him: for there be more with us than with him: With him is an arm of flesh; but with us is the Lord our God to help us, and to fight our battles. And the people rested themselves upon the words of Hezekiah king of Judah"* (2 Chronicles 32:7-8).

Hezekiah understood something everyone needs to realize: when you trust in flesh you can only have what flesh can produce. But when you place your trust in the Lord you will receive what God can produce.

- The Lord performs miracles while man performs the mundane.
- God performs the extraordinary while man performs the ordinary.

Without question, I will take what the Almighty gives. Instead of having confidence in my own weak flesh, I will trust in the Lord.

By the way, after all of the threats of Sennacherib and his army, after the letter writing campaign designed to induce fear and panic had ended, God dispatched an angel to defeat Assyria and Sennacherib. Hezekiah won the victory because he trusted in the arm of the Lord. *"Some nations boast of their armies and weapons, but we boast in the Lord our God"* (Psalm 20:7 NLT).

ARE YOU LISTENING?

Make the right choice; listen to the right voice.

Do not let the dragon of self-sufficiency cause you to slip into a state of mediocrity and complacency that will ultimately result in your demise.

Listen instead to the voice of the Spirit as He

prepares you for the victory God has planned for you.

The dragon will whisper, "You will be okay on your own."

This is a lie. You will only be victorious through the power of the Holy Spirit working in your life.

SEVEN

THE DRAGON OF DOUBT

Again and again the enemy will suggest, "The future looks bleak. Why don't you just give up."

At every turn, this dragon is sowing seeds of discouragement and doubt. What is the antidote? It is found in a five letter word called *faith.*

There are three facts we need to establish regarding this God-given necessity:

First: Faith is necessary.

The passage of scripture which speaks volumes to me of the absolute need for faith is when Jesus said, *"Simon, Simon, Satan has asked to sift you as wheat. But I have prayed for you, Simon, that your faith may not fail. And when you have turned back, strengthen your brothers"* (Luke 22:31-32 NIV).

This conversation with Simon Peter is an amazing exchange.

Jesus is concerned for Peter's future. He knows how much Satan would like to destroy this disciple and stop his influence before he can make his mark for the kingdom.

The Lord is trying to get through to this man who thinks he is nearly invincible and convince him that the days ahead would be very rough indeed.

Peter would find out soon enough how quickly you can be rattled when things don't go as planned. Jesus knew Peter was about to face the most tumultuous moments of his life. Not only this, but the Lord was spending some of His last minutes before Calvary with His beloved disciple.

JESUS' VITAL PRAYER

In this hour of warning and compassion, during the moments when the pressure was mounting, Jesus made this statement to Simon Peter: "I have prayed for you." But what was His prayer?

Personally, I think when the events of God's Son were coming to a head on this earth, and when the days ahead would be the toughest Peter ever experienced, I believe Jesus would only pray for what was most important. Notice, Jesus prayed that Peter's "faith may not fail."

- He did not pray that Peter's ability to preach the message would not fail him, even though he would need this ability on the day of Pentecost and beyond.
- He did not pray that his strength would not waver, even though I'm sure the days ahead were an unbelievable test of strength and fortitude.
- He did not pray that Peter would have enough money to carry out his ministry, even though he would also need resources.

No, Jesus did not utter any of the hundreds of prayers He could have. At the very end of His earthly journey with Peter, when the pressure was on, Jesus offered the most important prayer—for a faith which would not falter or fail.

This is vital, because in the final analysis all we really need is faith.

THE MOST VALUABLE POSSESSION

Peter would preach, possess strength to overcome his failure, and have the means to carry on his ministry, because he still had belief, expectation and trust in God.

I have come to the conclusion that it is of utmost importance that you and I have and cherish this vital possession.

You can be stripped of everything else in life, but if you have faith you can get it all back.

If I have to make a choice, the world can take everything except this one thing:

- Take my car and I will get another one if I still have my faith.
- Burn my house; I will build another one if my faith remains.
- Steal my clothes; I can replace them if I have faith.
- Try to remove all reason to hope from me and I will still hope because I have faith and belief.

Just give me my faith and I will make it.

Second: It doesn't take a whole lot of faith.

Once, when Jesus was with His disciples, a crowd formed and a man who was in great distress approached the Lord, telling Him how his son was tortured by an evil spirit which jeopardized the boy's life. He cried, *"Lord, have mercy on my son...He has seizures and is suffering greatly. He often falls into the fire or into the water"* (Matthew 17:15 NIV).

The disciples, it appears, had tried to help but were unable to heal the young man.

When Jesus heard this story He quickly delivered

the boy from the demon which had tortured him. Then, the disciples came to the Lord privately and asked, "Why couldn't we drive the devils out?"

MUSTARD SEED FAITH

Jesus used the opportunity to teach them a simple lesson. He answered, *"Because you have so little faith. I tell you the truth, if you have faith as small as a mustard seed, you can say to this mountain, 'Move from here to there' and it will move. Nothing will be impossible for you"* (Matthew 17:20 NIV).

In those days the mustard seed was proverbial for smallness. If you really wanted to stress the point that something was tiny you would do so by comparing it to this extremely small seed. Jesus was telling them that if we have even a minuscule portion of faith we can accomplish great things.

Mustard seed faith is all it takes to move the mountains of life. So, it's not really important that we have a huge reservoir filled with belief. Rather, we only need *some* faith—even a small amount. As a result, we can do significant things for Christ.

Third: You must recognize and utilize the faith you have.

In order to speak to monumental problems and tell them to move you need to recognize that faith is alive in you. It's the key to believing the promise of Jesus: "Nothing will be impossible for you."

Right now you may be saying, "I wish I had some faith."

I have very good news. You do! Silence the dragon that is speaking to you, trying to convince you that you don't have any, because I am about to prove him wrong. In fact, the faith needed for every situation you will ever face has already been provided.

Pay close attention to these words of the apostle Paul: *"For I say, through the grace given unto me, to every man that is among you, not to think of himself more highly than he ought to think; but to think soberly, according as God hath dealt to every man the measure of faith"* (Romans 12:3).

There it is! You *do* possess faith!

HE KNOWS WHAT LIES AHEAD

If the assignment of measuring out what was needed for my life were left to anyone else, I couldn't be confident I would actually have enough to make it through. But we are talking about the almighty God, who knows just what I need and has provided the faith necessary.

The Creator has an eternal view and is never caught off guard or taken by surprise.

You will never find God over in the corner curled up in a fetal position because some unexpected event occurred. With your heavenly Father there is no future and no past; He lives in an eternal present. It is always "right now" with God. He declares, *"I make known the end from the beginning, from ancient times, what is still to come. I say: My purpose will stand, and I will do all that I please"* (Isaiah 46:10 NIV).

My interpretation of this verse is very simple: God sees everything at once and He does whatever He pleases. You see, time means nothing to Him. As scripture states, *"But, beloved, be not ignorant of this one thing, that one day is with the Lord as a thousand years, and a thousand years as one day"* (2 Peter 3:8).

Our God, who sees the conclusion from the start and knows everything we will go through, is the same One who measures out the faith to every man. If the Lord knew what I would encounter before I ever breathed my first breath, don't you think He would give me enough faith to cover every circumstance and situation? I do.

THERE'S ENOUGH!

Picture this. God is in heaven with a pitcher in His hand. He is pouring faith into the reservoir of your soul and is making sure you have an ample supply to sustain you through life:

- The Lord sees the broken relationship and has already given you the faith to repair the rift.

- God is observing your protracted illness and is supplying ample faith for your healing.
- He sees the dry season when you just can't seem to feel His presence and He provides the faith to keep believing.
- Your heavenly Father knows when your child isn't behaving right and gives you faith to press on.
- God sees the almost unbearable grief at the loss of a loved one and measures out a little more faith for you.
- He knows when someone mistreats you, perhaps even in the church, and will make sure your faith won't let you quit.
- The Lord understood your new job would be just a little over your head, so He gave you enough faith to last until you learned what to do.
- God knew before it happened that the trouble you are now in would come your way and He gave you faith to cover it all.

According to the Word, I can promise the Lord will

never leave you empty handed. Your faith tank may not be overflowing, but there is enough to get the job done.

This is why you can stand to your feet and confidently declare, "Get thee behind me, dragon. I do have faith. And nothing will be impossible for me!"

EIGHT

THE DRAGON OF ISOLATION

Several years ago scientists discovered what they believe to be the oldest and largest living creature on planet earth. Perhaps as you read this statement you are tempted to make a guess. Contrary to what you may be thinking, this creature is not a blue whale; it is not a giant redwood tree—nor is it your 9th grade Algebra teacher! But, it is something known as *Armillaria bulbosa.*

Leonard Sweet describes it in his book *Faithquakes* as a mass of subterranean cytoplasm that feeds off of rotting organic matter and tree roots. This blob is estimated to be more than 1,500 years old and weighs as much as 1,000 tons.

The place which is the residence of this giant fungus is my home state Michigan. Here, we really do not have a long list to brag about. We don't have balmy weather or a Disney theme park, and as I write, we don't even have a championship football team. But when it comes to fungi, we can boast the largest in the world!

Crystal Falls, Michigan, is a town of about 2,000 way up in Northern Michigan a few hundred miles from our home in the suburbs of Detroit.

According to Sweet, Crystal Falls is coming to terms with its new identity with mushroom burgers, fungus fudge, mushroom festivals, and tee shirts which proclaim: "A Humongous Fungus is Among Us."

I understand that if you visit the area you may see an individual mushroom spring forth from the earth, but if you think it is one single isolated and shallow rooted fungus, you have likely made a mistake. It is not alone. The single mushroom in the field is the product of this "Armillaria bulbosa." It is a part of something very deep, very old and very large.

ARE YOU ALONE?

A dragon many people face is one that makes you

feel as though you walking through life all by yourself. If not dealt with, this dangerous force will drive you to isolation and will become a self-fulfilling prophesy.

It seems this particular problem is one many committed believers seem to constantly battle with. It brings with it the thought that no one really loves you and that people are not really concerned for your welfare.

This dragon tries to make you feel like one single, solitary, isolated mushroom, when the truth is you are not alone.

You are connected to the body of Christ, the local church, and even better, the Lord Jesus Christ. Wow! What a connection!

Your divine link is old, deep and large. You are joined to the 2,000 year old New Testament church and every one who names the name of Christ living on earth now and those who are in the grave. You are not alone—and never will be!

If somehow the enemy of your soul thinks he can

target and pick you off easily, because on the surface it seems you have no connection, he will be making a terrible mistake.

When this dragon assaults you, he attacks the body of Christ and almighty God.

Needless to say, this will be more of a fight than he ever anticipated.

A MAN NAMED SHAMGAR

You have connections which extend far beyond what the eye can see, and scripture amplifies the point. In the book of Judges we read, *"And after him [Ehud] was Shamgar the son of Anath, which slew of the Philistines six hundred men with an ox goad: and he also delivered Israel"* (Judges 3:31).

You may be wondering, "Shamgar? Who is he?"

Unlike Moses, Abraham, David, Peter and Paul, Shamgar is not a greatly quoted or widely known biblical character. At first glance it seems that Shamgar is an insignificant farmer. He is only mentioned twice in the Bible; once in the above verse and the other instance is in Deborah's song recorded in Judges 5:6.

There it states, *"In the days of Shamgar the son of Anath, in the days of Jael, the highways were unoccupied, and the travellers walked through byways."*

Times had become so bad for the nation of Judah that they were easy prey for whoever wanted to invade and steal from them. The part of the country which lay next to the Philistines was so infested with plunderers, the people could not even travel the roads in safety. To journey on a highway or a main road in the days of Shamgar would be to take a chance with your very life. Even if you were not killed you would almost certainly be robbed.

The people of Judah, it seems, had no weapons; they had been disarmed. So they lived in guarded cities and sought shelter in fortified villages. If you were in the market to purchase a house in Shamgar's day you would only buy one in a well-protected area.

It was in this terrible situation we find Shamgar. He was unarmed, unguarded, out in the country all by himself. When the Philistines saw him they thought he was just one guy out there in his field alone with no connections, unprotected—so they attacked.

THEY UNDERESTIMATED HIM

Shamgar wasn't looking for trouble. Nor was he trying to be some kind of national hero seeking fame and notoriety. He was just minding his own business, cultivating his field and trying to take care of his family. Then, as we read in Judges 3, he was attacked.

The Bible does not tell us exactly how it happened. We don't know if the enemy pounced one at a time at first, or if they started with a small regiment, or if all 600 came and jumped him at once. All I know is that when the cloud of dust had settled, Shamgar was standing in the middle of his field with an ox goad in his hand and 600 Philistines lay lifeless on the ground.

They underestimated this farmer because despite what it may have looked like, he was not alone. The almighty God was on his side. Yes, Shamgar had heavenly connections!

SERVE NOTICE!

Be courageous and come against the dragon that

tries to confuse your mind, the one who tells you that you will never be victorious because you are too insignificant.

Confront this trick of the enemy of your soul because, remember, you are never alone.

Serve notice to the devil, doubters, and dragons: "If you are coming against me you may want to reconsider because I am connected and have a source of strength and power you do not see. I am not alone, never have been and never will be."

The Word assures you, *"Now ye are the body of Christ, and members in particular"* (1 Corinthians 12:27).

The word *particular* is translated from the Greek term "meros"—which means "section, piece, portion, or a division."

So Paul is saying we are a section of the body of Christ. This is good news because if someone hurts you they hurt all believers, and if the devil wants to fight you he has to take on the whole body of Christ.

You are not a lonely solitary soul; you are joined to

Jehovah God. His entire being—in heaven and on earth—is with you and you will be victorious.

BACK FROM THE TOMBS

The fascinating thing about this "All Alone" dragon is that it talks to people until eventually they act out in real life what he has implanted in their mind. If this thought is allowed to go unchecked it will eventually drive a person to the place where they are completely isolated. This removal from fellowship is a dangerous place to be.

It is obvious that the ultimate aim of the devil is to drive you to reclusiveness so you will not be able to hear the voices of reason—then he can fill your thoughts with whatever evil he chooses.

DESPERATE FOR FELLOWSHIP

The demoniac of Gadera (Mark 5) is a prime example of this. It is interesting to note that the evil spirits drove this man to the tombs. It was a lonely place where there was no one to speak into his life. There, he spun completely out of control.

Eventually, he was bound, but he could break the best ropes and the strongest chains. It appears that people were so afraid they would not go near him.

I'm sure this man was desperate to try and take charge of his life. After all, who would want to live this animal like existence? But the evil spirits, his isolation, and his surroundings kept him from gaining control.

Then one day, when everyone had given up on him—and no doubt he had given up on himself—a boat came bobbing along the seashore. And there at the seaside cemetery, Jesus showed up to give the man victory over his life again.

Many amazing things happened on that day. Jesus sent the demons fleeing from the tortured man into a herd of pigs that were feeding nearby. The pigs ran off a cliff and fell to their death. The man recovered his senses and the townspeople were amazed.

After his deliverance, *"When Jesus got back into the boat, the man who had been demon possessed begged to go, too"* (Mark 5:18 NLT).

Prior to all of this, he sought the isolation and despair of the tombs—and the devil also wanted him there. But as soon as he gained control of his mind, he desired fellowship.

Do not live alone. Don't fall for the dragon's deceptive lies and allow his prophecy to be fulfilled in your life.

God has a far better plan.

NINE

THE DRAGON OF PAST MISTAKES

T he apostle Paul penned the following words to the church in Corinth, and they knew exactly where he was coming from: *"Therefore judge nothing before the time, until the Lord come, who both will bring to light the hidden things of darkness, and will make manifest the counsels of the hearts: and then shall every man have praise of God"* (1 Corinthians 4:5).

Nobody else could understand this concept of waiting before deciding the final fate of someone or someplace like the people of Corinth. To better explain, let's take a look into the history of this Greek city—which lies about 50 miles west of Athens.

Corinth was a major commercial port, and because of its location became a crossroads for trade. The city was called "The Bridge of Greece" because, the north to south traffic of the nation passed through it as well as the east to west trade of the Mediterranean. Since a vast quantity of goods came through Corinth, most of the objects of luxury could be found in the market. These factors all converged to make this city a rich and populous place.

However, in 146 BC, disaster struck this proud and prosperous ancient city. The Romans were engaged in conquering the world and they marched right through Corinth.

General Lucius Mummius captured the city and left it a desolate heap of ruins. The once formidable Corinth lay in a state of ill repair for nearly one hundred years. Then, in 46 BC, Julius Caesar rebuilt the city and she arose from the ruins to become a very powerful capital once more.

By the time of Paul's missionary journeys, Corinth had regained her place of commercial supremacy.

So when Paul brings the message to hold off on judgment until the Lord has completed His work, these people knew exactly what he was talking about. They had risen to the top, fallen to the depths, and back up to the top again!

IT'S TOO EARLY!

Allow me to caution you concerning the dangers of judging the effects of your life before the entire story can be told. What looks like a failure today can be a tremendous success story tomorrow.

The dragon may be telling you it is all over and that you will never rise from the devastation of your past, but I am here to assure you it is not finished until God says so! It is tempting to judge hastily, but in doing so, the pronouncement is often wrong.

Don't let the dragon prematurely convince you of quitting. It is too early—and the Lord has not yet completed His work.

The hidden things have yet to be revealed, and your heart has not yet been bathed in light. According to the Word, everything will look different when the brightness of the Lord begins to shine.

WAIT AWHILE!

Think of how foolish it would be to size up some of the greatest athletes who have ever played on a ball field or graced a basketball court by one less-than-perfect season. You see, no one enters the Hall of Fame based on one good year, nor is one kept out because of a horrible year. The decision for such an honor is not made until a career is completely over.

Reggie Jackson became known as "Mr. October" for his late season and playoff baseball heroics, but just about everyone has forgotten that he also struck out more than 2,500 times in his career.

Lou Brock is heralded for the hitting, base stealing Hall-of-Famer he was—and with more than 3,000 hits and 938 stolen bases he deserves the recognition. But he also struck out over 1,700 times! It's a good thing managers and owners did not give up because of a few rough "at bats."

Michael Jordan is touted by most as the greatest basketball player to ever play the game. When we talk about "Air Jordan" we celebrate the 12,192 shots he made and usually forget the 12,537 shots he missed. Remember, a few errant shots do not ruin a distinguished career.

To evaluate any of these players at the start would have been a mistake. Conversely, to only look at the strikeouts and missed shots would also be a grave injustice.

————— ❧ —————

Some things just cannot be judged until the final game.

THE LAST CHAPTER

Just think how unfair it would have been to critique some of the most incredible characters in the Bible by only one season in their lives.

If you wrote the record of Jonah when he boarded the boat to Tarshish you would have said he was disobedient to the voice of the Lord and a complete failure, but you would have been wrong. You can't completely make an assessment of his life by the events in the first chapter of Jonah. To get it right you have to wait until the end of the book. Combine all of Jonah's disobedience and bad attitude with his repentance and preaching and you will have the complete picture. Anything short of a decision based on his entire life would be in error.

HEAR THE WHOLE STORY

Take Samson, for example. If you sized him up after he was captured by the Philistines, and formed your opinion on a short span of time, you would miss the entire history of the man. It would be unfair to judge him solely on the fact he was captured, imprisoned and blinded. Because he was at one point directionless, without vision, and the laughingstock of his enemies does not tell the whole story.

One day Samson left the mill where he had spent a season in his life and achieved his greatest victory—when most people had already written him off. To leave Samson at the Philistine's mill would be to appraise him before his time.

WHAT DOES GOD SAY?

If you wrote your opinion of David exclusively on his illicit affair with Bathsheba (and then the subsequent lying and murder), it would be understandable if you thought he was a man so far removed from God he would never be used in the Kingdom. But to do this would be a mistake.

The rest of the record had yet to be written, and time had not run out for him.

His season of adultery, murder and dishonesty was certainly a terrible era, but when God looked at the whole picture he did not quickly tag David as a failure. Instead, He called him, *"a man after mine own heart"* (Acts 13:22).

HOLD YOUR APPRAISAL

It would be untimely to decide how the life of Peter would be remembered just after he had denied the Lord three times. If you wrote his biography in those moments when he is warming himself by an open fire and swearing that he was no follower of Jesus—you would be incorrect. Be patient. Wait a while! Hold your judgment until Jesus calls him back into service at a seaside meeting. Wait until he preaches on the day of Pentecost, or until he is martyred for the cause of Christ. Only then can you make an accurate assessment of Peter's time on earth.

SUNDAY IS COMING!

When Jesus was crucified and laid in a tomb it looked like death had conquered Him. If you would have passed judgment on the Friday He died on the cross, your analysis would be premature. Even if you were to assess the situation on Saturday you still wouldn't have the complete picture.

In order to see the power of Jesus Christ over death, hell, and the grave you have to wait until early Sunday morning when an angel is sitting in an empty tomb looking at the grave clothes that had once covered Jesus' body. You just can't write the entire story until the third day.

FROM PERSECUTOR TO PREACHER

No one knew the power of this lesson better than the apostle Paul. When writing to the Corinthians, he is speaking of something he had learned from personal experience.

Paul had been an aggressive persecutor of the early

church. He was zealous and did his work well. But if you were to make your decision based on the early years of his life you would have it wrong. Why? Because Paul had a Damascus Road experience, and looking up into a blinding light he heard the voice of Jesus that changed his future forever.

From that moment on Paul went from being the persecutor *of* the church to being the apostle *to* the church. This is why he could preach the message more effectively than anyone: "Judge nothing before the time."

Do not allow this dragon of past mistakes to convince you that just because you have hit a bump in the road your destination is in jeopardy. Tell him, and anyone else who will listen, "I will not judge my life by merely one season. There are victories waiting ahead."

With God's guidance, it will be a marvelous story.

TEN

THE DRAGON
OF UNCERTAINTY

W hether we want to admit it or not, all of us have fought bouts with the dragon of self-doubt. It is particularly powerful and enters your life breathing fire, intimidation, and speaking disaster to your mind. The message is simple, yet hard to ignore: "You are not good enough, powerful enough, or connected enough for God to use."

The feeling which accompanies this thinking causes you to question and doubt: "Sure God can use just about anybody, but He cannot use me. I am insignificant. I do not count in the Kingdom."

Some have dealt with this more successfully than others, but we have all had to go one-on-one with debilitating thoughts from time to time. It is important to understand that everybody—even the spiritual giant, the faith healer, your grandmother; everybody —has encountered this dragon. So, be prepared for a head-on confrontation and make up your mind that you are not backing down.

A BIRTH OF COURAGE

History is replete with examples of men and women who achieved the extraordinary in spite of their apparent inabilities. Some of these individuals accomplished their greatness for selfish purposes, others for fame, wealth, to help the world, and some because of love.

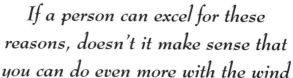

If a person can excel for these reasons, doesn't it make sense that you can do even more with the wind of the will of God at your back?

As I see it, if you obey the Lord's call and do the work of the Father, nothing will be outside of your ability.

The Lord specializes in taking the least likely man or woman and using them to do great exploits for His glory. Even as you read these words, I pray you will experience the birth of courage and faith in your heart. If God will do this for one person, He will do it for everyone.

Consider the words of the apostle Peter: *"I now realize how true it is that God does not show favoritism"* (Acts 10:34 NIV). Our loving heavenly Father not only works through people who lived thousands of years ago in Bible times; the scripture teaches us that Jesus Christ is the same yesterday, today, and forever (Hebrews 13:8).

THINK WHAT IS POSSIBLE

When this dragon of uncertainty attempts to derail the work you are called to do, remind him of these examples from the Word:

David

From the smallest Sunday school child to the oldest adult, we have all celebrated David's amazing victory over Goliath. Without question, this is a tremendous example of the power of God to help you even when the odds are not in your favor. Who wouldn't be inspired by this account of a shepherd boy bringing triumph to a nation as he defeats a giant who is a trained warrior?

However, we should remember that when the prophet Samuel came to anoint a king, David was not originally considered for the position. David's father, Jesse, failed to see the potential in his own son, and instead sent David's seven brothers out to meet Samuel.

David was not chosen by his earthly father, rather he was the choice of his heavenly Father.

Thank God the shepherd boy did not listen to self-doubt.

Gideon

A man named Gideon is lauded because he led a

small army of just 300 Israelites to victory over the Midianites. But perhaps the greatest triumph Gideon ever won was over his own uncertainty and lack of confidence.

When God called him to this monumental task of delivering the nation of Israel, Gideon immediately began to tell the Lord why he wasn't the man for the assignment. *"How and with what could I ever save Israel? Look at me. My clan's the weakest in Manasseh and I'm the runt of the litter"* (Judges 6:15 TM).

Gideon soon discovered how God can take even the least, for His best!

Christ Jesus

Over the hills of Bethlehem, the night sky lit up and angels appeared to proclaim the good news of the birth of the Savior. You would think this heavenly display would appear to the influential political leaders of the day, but it did not. Surely God must have arranged this announcement for the religious leaders of Israel. After all, they could have taken the message back to the temple where it would have spread like wildfire through the Jewish world, but this did not happen either.

No, God did not choose to make the announcement to the wealthy, nor the influential. Instead, He heralded the coming of the Messiah to the lowly shepherds. The Bible records:

And there were in the same country shepherds abiding in the field, keeping watch over their flock by night. And, lo, the angel of the Lord came upon them, and the glory of the Lord shone round about them: and they were sore afraid. And the angel said unto them, Fear not: for, behold, I bring you good tidings of great joy, which shall be to all people. For unto you is born this day in the city of David a Saviour, which is Christ the Lord.

And this shall be a sign unto you; Ye shall find the babe wrapped in swaddling clothes, lying in a manger. And suddenly there was with the angel a multitude of the heavenly host praising God, and saying, Glory to God in the highest, and on earth peace, good will toward men. And it came to pass, as the angels were gone away from them into heaven, the shepherds said one to another, Let us now go even unto Bethlehem, and see this thing which is come to pass, which the Lord hath made known unto us. And they came with haste, and found Mary, and Joseph, and the babe lying in a manger. And when they had seen it, they made known abroad the saying which was told them concerning this child (Luke 2:8-17).

God used ordinary people to reveal the birth of the Savior of the world. If the single most important event in history was shared with common men, then God must specialize in working with the seemingly humble and insignificant.

ARE YOU AVAILABLE?

When a crowd of 5,000 who had stayed to hear the teachings of Jesus became hungry, the Lord wanted to provide a meal for them. He took the lunch of one young boy and multiplied it to feed the entire throng (Mark 6:30-44).

115

If the Son of God can cause such a divine increase with five meager loaves of bread and two small fish, it stands to reason He can take your talents and abilities and use them for His glory. All that is required is the desire to make yourself available for His purpose.

This story carries with it a vital truth. God is in the business of meeting the needs of humanity and He can use anyone and anything to accomplish the mission.

Please understand, however, that when the Lord uses you, it is not your opportunity to be consumed with pride, because the event is not really about you. It concerns human need, the power of God, and how He can use an available vessel:

- Jesus knows how to take mud and make medicine that will restore eyesight.
- He can use a simple stable and a lowly manger to house the King of kings and Lord of lords.
- Jesus can use a rugged wooden cross to save mankind.
- He can use a borrowed tomb to shine the light of hope all over the world.
- God knows how to make a staff roll back the Red Sea and cause water to flow out of a rock.

- The Lord can deliver His transforming message through an angel, or a servant girl.
- He can send an anointed prophet, or He can speak through a donkey.
- God can quiet a howling storm with just a word.
- He can use a small Upper Room in Jerusalem as the headquarters for the beginning of a massive world wide revival.

The Lord will take whatever and whoever is available to do the work of God on earth. If the Almighty can do all of this through those He chooses, He can and *will* use you.

Please do not miss out on the glorious destiny God has planned for your life. Don't let the dragon of self-doubt manipulate you into becoming less than your heavenly Father envisions.

You *can* do all things through Christ who gives you confidence, authority and His divine strength.

"ONE MINUTE" DRAGON SLAYERS

T ime and space does not permit us to cover in full detail every dragon that the human mind encounters. There are as many as there are different imaginations in the thoughts of man.

We have discussed several, including the dragons of anger, deceit, doubt, isolation, past mistakes and uncertainty. However, on the following pages you will find additional enemies you need to conquer. Most important, I want you to use the scriptures to refute these foes.

The heroes of the faith are those who courageously confront and slay dragons with the Word of God. Let's get started:

Slay the dragon of death.

"Yea, though I walk through the valley of the

shadow of death, I will fear no evil: for thou art with me; thy rod and thy staff they comfort me" (Psalm 23:4).

"Verily, verily, I say unto you, If a man keep my saying, he shall never see death" (John 8:51).

"For I am persuaded, that neither death, nor life, nor angels, nor principalities, nor powers, nor things present, nor things to come, Nor height, nor depth, nor any other creature, shall be able to separate us from the love of God, which is in Christ Jesus our Lord" (Romans 8:38-39).

Slay the dragon of discontent.

"Let not thine heart envy sinners: but be thou in the fear of the Lord all the day long" (Proverbs 23:17).

"I will greatly rejoice in the Lord, my soul shall be joyful in my God; for he hath clothed me with the garments of salvation, he hath covered me with the robe of righteousness, as a bridegroom decketh *himself with ornaments, and as a bride adorneth herself with her jewels. For as the earth bringeth forth her bud, and as the garden causeth the things that are sown in it to spring forth; so the Lord God will cause righteousness and praise to spring forth before all the nations"* (Isaiah 61:10-11).

Slay the dragon of discouragement.

"There shall not any man be able to stand before thee all the days of thy life: as I was with Moses, so I will be with thee: I will not fail thee, nor forsake thee" (Joshua 1:5).

"Why art thou cast down, O my soul? and why art thou disquieted within me? hope thou in God: for I shall yet praise him, who is the health of my countenance, and my God" (Psalm 42:11).

Slay the dragon of disobedience.

"O that there were such an heart in them, that they would fear me, and keep all my commandments always, that it might be well with them, and with their children for ever!" (Deuteronomy 5:29).

"*He that keepeth the commandment keepeth his own soul; but he that despiseth his ways shall die*" (Proverbs 19:16).

"*Whosoever transgresseth, and abideth not in the doctrine of Christ, hath not God. He that abideth in the doctrine of Christ, he hath both the Father and the Son*" (2 John 1:9).

Slay the dragon of distress.

"*Rest in the Lord, and wait patiently for him: fret not thyself because of him who prospereth in his way, because of the man who bringeth wicked devices to pass*" (Psalm 37:7).

"*Tribulation and anguish, upon every soul of man that doeth evil...But glory, honour, and peace, to every man that worketh good*" (Romans 2:9-10).

"*For our light affliction, which is but for a moment, worketh for us a far more exceeding and eternal weight of glory; While we look not at the things which are seen, but at the things which are not* seen: for the things which are seen are temporal; but the things which are not seen are eternal" (2 Corinthians 4:17-18).

Slay the dragon of distrust.

"They that trust in the Lord shall be as mount Zion, which cannot be removed, but abideth for ever" (Psalm 125:1).

"Trust in the Lord with all thine heart; and lean not unto thine own understanding. In all thy ways acknowledge him, and he shall direct thy paths" (Proverbs 3:5-6).

Slay the dragon of fear.

"Be not afraid of sudden fear, neither of the desolation of the wicked, when it cometh. For the Lord shall be thy confidence, and shall keep thy foot from being taken" (Proverbs 3:25-26).

"In righteousness shalt thou be established: thou shalt be far from oppression; for thou shalt not fear: and from terror; for it shall not come near thee" (Isaiah 54:14).

"For ye have not received the spirit of bondage again to fear; but ye have received the Spirit of adoption, whereby we cry, Abba, Father"(Romans 8:15).

Slay the dragon of guilt.

"As far as the east is from the west, so far hath he removed our transgressions from us" (Psalm 103:12).

"Let the wicked forsake his way, and the unrighteous man his thoughts: and let him return unto the Lord, and he will have mercy upon him; and to our God, for he will abundantly pardon" (Isaiah 55:7).

"And I will cleanse them from all their iniquity, whereby they have sinned against me; and I will pardon all their iniquities, whereby they have sinned, and whereby they have transgressed against me"(Jeremiah 33:8).

Slay the dragon of impatience.

"And let us not be weary in well doing: for in due season we shall reap, if we faint not" (Galatians 6:9).

"That ye be not slothful, but followers of them who through faith and patience inherit the promises" (Hebrews 6:12).

"Be patient therefore, brethren, unto the coming of the Lord. Behold, the husbandman waiteth for the precious fruit of the earth, and hath long patience for it, until he receive the early and latter rain. Be ye also patient; stablish your hearts: for the coming of the Lord draweth nigh" (James 5:7-8).

Slay the dragon of insecurity.

"Keep me as the apple of the eye, hide me under the shadow of thy wings, From the wicked that oppress me, from my deadly enemies, who compass me about" (Psalm 17:8-9).

"Thou art my hiding place; thou shalt preserve me

from trouble; thou shalt compass me about with songs of deliverance" (Psalm 32:7).

Slay the dragon of jealousy.

"Let not thine heart envy sinners: but be thou in the fear of the Lord all the day long. For surely there is an end; and thine expectation shall not be cut off" (Proverbs 23:17-18).

"Let us not be desirous of vain glory, provoking one another, envying one another" (Galatians 5:26).

Slay the dragon of laziness.

"He that tilleth his land shall have plenty of bread: but he that followeth after vain persons shall have poverty enough" (Proverbs 28:19).

"Let him that stole steal no more: but rather let him labour, working with his hands the thing which is good, that he may have to give to him that needeth" (Ephesians 4:28).

"And that ye study to be quiet, and to do your own

business, and to work with your own hands, as we commanded you; That ye may walk honestly toward them that are without, and that ye may have lack of nothing"(1 Thessalonians 4:11-12).

Slay the dragon of negative thinking.

"Jesus said unto him, Thou shalt love the Lord thy God with all thy heart, and with all thy soul, and with all thy mind"(Matthew 22:37).

"And be not conformed to this world: but be ye transformed by the renewing of your mind, that ye may prove what is that good, and acceptable, and perfect, will of God"(Romans 12:2).

"Finally, brethren, whatsoever things are true, whatsoever things are honest, whatsoever things are just, whatsoever things are pure, whatsoever things are lovely, whatsoever things are of good report; if there be any virtue, and if there be any praise, think on these things"(Philippians 4:8).

Slay the dragon of poverty.

"And I will send grass in thy fields for thy cattle,

that thou mayest eat and be full" (Deuteronomy 11:15).

"And it shall come to pass, if thou shalt hearken diligently unto the voice of the Lord thy God, to observe and to do all his commandments which I command thee this day, that the Lord thy God will set thee on high above all nations of the earth: And all these blessings shall come on thee, and overtake thee" (Deuteronomy 28:1-2).

"And the Lord thy God will make thee plenteous in every work of thine hand, in the fruit of thy body, and in the fruit of thy cattle, and in the fruit of thy land, for good" (Deuteronomy 30:9).

Slay the dragon of pride.

"A man's pride shall bring him low: but honour shall uphold the humble in spirit"(Proverbs 29:23).

"Whosoever therefore shall humble himself as this little child, the same is greatest in the kingdom of heaven"(Matthew 18:4).

"And whosoever shall exalt himself shall be abased; and he that shall humble himself shall be exalted" (Matthew 23:12).

Slay the dragon of selfishness.

"Let no man seek his own, but every man another's wealth" (1 Corinthians 10:24).

"Look not every man on his own things, but every man also on the things of others" (Philippians 2:4).

"Bear ye one another's burdens, and so fulfil the law of Christ" (Galatians 6:2).

Slay the dragon of sexual sins.

"Flee fornication. Every sin that a man doeth is without the body; but he that committeth fornication sinneth against his own body. What? know ye not that your body is the temple of the Holy Ghost which is in you, which ye have of God, and ye are not your own? For ye are bought with a price: therefore glorify God in your body, and in

your spirit, which are God's" (1 Corinthians 6:18-20).

"There hath no temptation taken you but such as is common to man: but God is faithful, who will not suffer you to be tempted above that ye are able; but will with the temptation also make a way to escape, that ye may be able to bear it" (1 Corinthians 10:13).

"Blessed is the man that endureth temptation: for when he is tried, he shall receive the crown of life, which the Lord hath promised to them that love him" (James 1:12).

Slay the dragon of shame.

"And hope maketh not ashamed; because the love of God is shed abroad in our hearts by the Holy Ghost which is given unto us" (Romans 5:5).

"For the scripture saith, Whosoever believeth on him shall not be ashamed" (Romans 10:11).

"For the which cause I also suffer these things: nevertheless I am not ashamed: for I know whom I have believed, and am persuaded that he is able to keep that which I have committed unto him against that day" (2 Timothy 1:12).

Slay the dragon of sickness.

"Heal me, O Lord, and I shall be healed; save me, and I shall be saved: for thou art my praise" (Jeremiah 17:14).

"Is any sick among you? let him call for the elders of the church; and let them pray over him, anointing him with oil in the name of the Lord: And the prayer of faith shall save the sick, and the Lord shall raise him up; and if he have committed sins, they shall be forgiven him" (James 5:14-15).

Slay the dragon of sin.

"Then will I sprinkle clean water upon you, and ye shall be clean: from all your filthiness, and from all your idols, will I cleanse you. A new heart also will I give you, and a new spirit will I put within you:

131

and I will take away the stony heart out of your flesh, and I will give you an heart of flesh" (Ezekiel 36:25-26).

"Therefore if any man be in Christ, he is a new creature: old things are passed away; behold, all things are become new"(2 Corinthians 5:17).

Slay the dragon of sorrow.

"Weeping may endure for a night, but joy cometh in the morning"(Psalm 30:5).

"And the ransomed of the Lord shall return, and come to Zion with songs and everlasting joy upon their heads: they shall obtain joy and gladness, and sorrow and sighing shall flee away"(Isaiah 35:10).

"And God shall wipe away all tears from their eyes; and there shall be no more death, neither sorrow, nor crying, neither shall there be any more pain: for the former things are passed away" (Revelation 21:4).

Slay the dragon of stinginess.

"The liberal soul shall be made fat: and he that watereth shall be watered also himself" (Proverbs 11:25).

"And the King shall answer and say unto them, Verily I say unto you, Inasmuch as ye have done it unto one of the least of these my brethren, ye have done it unto me" (Matthew 25:40).

"Give to every man that asketh of thee; and of him that taketh away thy goods ask them not again" (Luke 6:30).

Slay the dragon of gossip.

"Keep thy tongue from evil, and thy lips from speaking guile" (Psalm 34:13).

"Where no wood is, there the fire goeth out: so where there is no talebearer, the strife ceaseth. As coals are to burning coals, and wood to fire; so is a contentious man to kindle strife. The words of a talebearer are as wounds, and they go down into the innermost parts of the belly"(Proverbs 26-20-22).

Slay the dragon of unbelief.

"For God so loved the world, that he gave his only begotten Son, that whosoever believeth in him should not perish, but have everlasting life" (John 3:16).

"Jesus saith unto him, Thomas, because thou hast seen me, thou hast believed: blessed are they that have not seen, and yet have believed"(John 20:29).

Slay the dragon of unforgiveness.

"But I say unto you, Love your enemies, bless them that curse you, do good to them that hate you, and pray for them which despitefully use you, and persecute you" (Matthew 5:44).

"And when ye stand praying, forgive, if ye have ought against any: that your Father also which is in *heaven may forgive you your trespasses. But if ye do not forgive, neither will your Father which is in heaven forgive your trespasses"* (Mark 11:25-26).

Slay the dragon of unrighteousness.

"For the Lord God is a sun and shield: the LORD will give grace and glory: no good thing will he withhold from them that walk uprightly" (Psalm 84:11).

"The fear of the wicked, it shall come upon him: but the desire of the righteous shall be granted" (Proverbs 10:24).

"But seek ye first the kingdom of God, and his righteousness; and all these things shall be added unto you" (Matthew 6:33).

THE LIFE-CHANGING WORD

Picking up a Bible and reading a passage of scripture changes the atmosphere where it is read. Why? Because it changes you! And I believe Bible readers are the happiest people on earth.

You may have experienced some particular sorrow or hurt, or are living in a state of complete despair and have no idea of the next step to take. There is an answer. Turn to God's Word and start reading.

If you can't see clearly the solution to your problem, then at least you will find the story of someone else who long ago felt just like you. Before long you will be saying to yourself, "If these people can make it, if they can be used of God, so can I!

Suddenly, the atmosphere in the room seems different, but nothing has changed, except for you. The walls are still the same color, the carpet is waiting to be cleaned and the clutter needs to be picked up. The furniture is the same old stuff you have wanted to replace for a long time, but in this moment none of this seems important, because the Word has just transformed the world where you reside.

I am of the opinion that Christians today need to spend significantly more time in the Word and far less on the trivial activities which waste our lives. In the final analysis, it will not be the details we know about American Idol, the NFL, or world news that will give us hope. Rather, it will be what we have learned in

God's Word which lifts our spirits and brings expectation for a better tomorrow.

There are several portions of scripture that are brimming with victory and promise. Psalm 91 is one which speaks hope to my heart. Everything can go wrong, yet just one minute spent reading this psalm and I know things are going to be alright. It reconfirms to me how wonderful our God really is, how much He loves us, and how everything is in His control.

Take a moment to read this right now and I believe it will uplift your spirits also:

He that dwelleth in the secret place of the most High shall abide under the shadow of the Almighty. I will say of the Lord, He is my refuge and my fortress: my God; in him will I trust. Surely he shall deliver thee from the snare of the fowler, and from the noisome pestilence. He shall cover thee with his feathers, and under his wings shalt thou trust: his truth shall be thy shield and buckler. Thou shalt not be afraid for the terror by night; nor for the arrow that flieth by day; Nor for the pestilence that walketh in darkness; nor for the destruction that wasteth at noonday. A thousand shall fall at thy side, and ten thousand at thy right hand; but it shall not come nigh thee. Only with thine eyes shalt thou behold and see the reward of the wicked.

*B*ecause thou hast made the Lord, which is my refuge, even the most High, thy habitation; There shall no evil befall thee, neither shall any plague come nigh thy dwelling. For he shall give his angels charge over thee, to keep thee in all thy ways. They shall bear thee up in their hands, lest thou dash thy foot against a stone.

*T*hou shalt tread upon the lion and adder: the young lion and the dragon shalt thou trample under feet. Because he hath set his love upon me, therefore will I deliver him: I will set him on high, because he hath known my name. He shall call upon me, and I will answer him: I will be with him in trouble; I will deliver him, and honour him. With long life will I satisfy him, and shew him my salvation (Psalm 91:1-16).

I trust you already feel better, because this is more inspiring than any self-help book on the market. Just reading this puts a bright sun up against the clear blue skies of my future! Now I know everything will be alright, no matter what.

Let me share why this passage is so significant. Psalm 91 touches me on several levels. It tells me seven vital truths concerning my life and my relationship to the Lord:

1. God loves me.

This is the greatest revelation a man or woman can ever have. I am loved by God and am the apple of His eye.

2. Heaven is taking care of me.

I don't have to live my life always looking over my shoulder because I am not taking care of myself alone; I have heavenly help.

3. Hell cannot stop me.

"Take that Devil! No matter what you throw my

way, it won't work!" I can't lose unless I quit.

4. *The angels are watching over me.*

I have an army of defenders and protectors who cannot be seen. Day and night, angels are watching over me!

5. *My enemies are no match for me.*

The foes may come at me from one direction, but they will have to leave seven ways. No weapon formed against me shall prosper.

6. *God will answer me when I pray.*

For this reason I will keep on praying.

7. *I will see the salvation of the Lord.*

When I turn to Jesus, He turns to me.

START WALKING!

All of these divine favors from above are happening because I made the choice to sit down in the secret place of the "Most High" and abide under the shadow of the Almighty. I have learned it's significant where you are seated, because if you are in the proper place there is no end to the blessings.

This is exciting! It should also let you know that if you have totally surrendered your life to God and abide in His presence, you are "sitting pretty"—as the saying goes. You are in the refuge and fortress of your God with His faithfulness as your shield and His wings as your protection. You will not be terrorized by night or punctured with an arrow by day. You will not fall or be punished; instead, you will be safe and secure.

I rejoice in every word of this psalm and thank God for each precious promise it includes. But there is one verse in particular I want you to read aloud again and again until you can quote it in your sleep. Verse 13 is where we began this book: *"Thou shalt tread upon the lion and adder: the young lion and the dragon shalt thou trample under feet."*

With God's help, you can walk on dragons!

FOR A COMPLETE LIST OF RESOURCES
OR TO SCHEDULE THE AUTHOR
FOR SPEAKING ENGAGEMENTS,
CONTACT:

STEVE WARMAN
THE APOSTOLIC CHURCH
P.O. BOX 4385
AUBURN HILLS, MI 48321

PHONE: 248-373-4500